THE ADVANCED AGENT

How to increase profits, work less and scale your business faster

by **RICK GLADE**

Disclaimer

This content is not commissioned by the author. Any opinions, analyses, reviews or recommendations expressed in this book are those of the author alone, and may not have been reviewed, approved or otherwise endorsed by any other party. This book may suggest compensation based on the author's own experience and through third party relationships, systems and platforms known to the industry. This publication references performance and information collected over a multitude of years. Past results do not guarantee future results. All copyrights, logos, or monograms belong to their perspective owners and are not related in any way to the Advanced Agent. The Advanced Agent is a trademark of Rainy Day Ventures, LLC.

ISBN 978-0-9984918-3-7

Publisher Rainy Day Ventures, LLC Cheyenne, WY USA

Acknowledgments

I'd like to acknowledge Wilco Ravestijn for his collaboration in this book. I'd also like to acknowledge Matt Clark & Wes Longueira for the spark to make this book happen. I'd also like to thank my editing and graphics team and all of those who helped make this book come alive. And I'd like to thank all the raving fans of this book who wish to take their lives to a point of mastery on every level.

Dedication

This book is dedicated to every single agent out there looking to improve their way of life and to live more vibrantly. It's for those looking to make a bigger impact beyond just sales. To all those agents who followed my lead in becoming an Advanced Agent, I salute you and cherish your belief in me. I am honored to be your guide. You will now be the Advanced Agents of change who can make the greatest impact on an industry since the evolution of the internet.

Table of Contents:

Table of Contents:

Introduction:
Why I Wrote This Book

In my experience from being a leader in the real estate field for over 30 years and helping many people create long term wealth, I've discovered that it's best to give people what they want. The simple principle of "paying it forward" is why I wrote this book. While understanding it may not be apparent immediately, abundance flows through those who give and create value.

Keeping a mindset of what it takes to become an Advanced Agent is why this book is important for any real estate agent or broker wanting to increase their productivity, and more importantly, create a lifestyle of wealth by working with the most advanced and efficient tools, teams, and platforms available.

I, like most agents, started out with the idea this business was fairly simple. I thought it was as simple as getting a license and the very next day I would be making money. Wow, how I was in for a rude awakening! I thought it was all profit and little or no costs to doing business. The reality was I had to figure out how to make the best use of my time and also to figure out the best companies, platforms and tools to leverage the biggest bang for my buck! I not only wanted to maximize my ROI, but my ROT (return on time). It goes without saying TIME is our most valuable commodity for all of us. Time is more precious than money or gold. I knew I couldn't do it all, and it would take me several years to figure it all out on my own.

So, I wrote this book because I know success leaves clues and I personally believe failure leaves even more clues. I knew if I could share what has worked as well as what HASN'T worked. I would be doing a great service to many. Remember what I said about paying it forward? I am a firm believer in that theory! If I could just create a few short chapters and simplify the business for the masses of agents and brokers looking to scale their business quickly and with more than just one way to do it, I would have fulfilled my intentions as set out here.

Of course, you could continue on the same path you've been on and end up wherever that leads you. You can do as I did and continue struggling by trying every next best thing that is offered to you. For me, that meant just a bunch of motivational cul-de-sacs and over promised yet under delivered gimmicks. It meant spending more time away from my family and friends and truly kept me from doing the things that made me happy, which was quite frankly the ability to have enough deal flow and income to do absolutely nothing. Or better said, whatever I want –when I want – with whom I want.

So, I set off in search of the absolute best platforms in every aspect of the real estate business, knowing that technology is ever changing, and the business is always evolving. I wanted to use as much leverage as I could discover.

In just short of a year, I was able create a very successful momentum in my business. I was able to obtain absolutely more leads and scaled my business growth monthly, not just building but retaining a team of agents and taking back control of my time all while not radically changing my business model and, more importantly, with less overhead and effort.

I know, right here is where you are saying, "Okay, What's the catch? This can't be true. How can I receive more by doing less? How can doing less myself yield more money and time?" I am with you. Before I became an Advanced Agent, I was just as skeptical. It's all about using focused effort in the right places.

In these following chapters, you will read and discover exactly how I did it. What I discovered was my success was not only dependent on my efforts but applying those efforts in the right manner and using the right tools to leverage and scale those efforts by 10 times, and often as much as 100 times my own ability.

If you can identify with the struggle of the real estate business as much as I used to, you owe it to yourself to continue reading and see if you can put the power of the Advanced Agent into your business and create results faster, better, and more lucrative than you ever thought possible.

Are You Busy Yet Not Productive?

Most people are busier than ever, yet not productive. I used to be one of them. They say that "a dog that chases his tail will get dizzy." Many agents end up spending their energy chasing the business, always in a reactive mode rather than getting ahead and prospering. However, Advanced Agents set themselves up to be proactively successful. Instead of being one of the many, what if you could set yourself apart? Wouldn't it be nice to get ahead of the trends and plan for prosperity?

It's all about leverage and timing and having the insight to determine where things will be, rather than simply looking at where things are now. It's about the evolution of the world and business around you. Those who adjust their business mindset and adapt to the shifts in the market set themselves up to generate an incredible, thriving real estate business. You'll see how this is done throughout the experience and the case studies in this book.

If you've been in the real estate industry for four years or more, congratulations! You are part of the minority who have figured out how to survive in this business. But for those of you that say, "Just surviving is not good enough," I want you to stay tuned. Did you know that statistics from the National Association of Realtors shows a lot of agents don't even make it into their second year of doing this business? They simply give up because they didn't know where to turn for guidance or how to grow a real business. Real estate can be a very frustrating business. It can be very hard because until now it has always been based solely on sales and lead generation. This plan makes all agents equal because sales were the only avenue for income. We all understand that with this method, we are only as good as our last closed transaction.

Now here is your **first shift**: You can start to begin thinking about more than just survival from sales. I am going to show how Advanced Agents are constantly gaining beyond just sales. They have the possibility to add monthly income beyond their own efforts and potentially build a future exit strategy. Their productivity rewards them with monthly residual income and building assets for retirement.

We've all been stuck at one point or another. I was at this exact point in my own business. I always thought that to be successful, I needed to be self-employed as an agent and always be closing sales. Isn't the ABC (always be closing) method what they teach us? I eventually chose to make my real estate career more like that of an entrepreneur. I wanted to be more in control of the benefits from my efforts.

If you are like most real estate professionals, you can't step away from your own business. Your business really is just a job that employs you. Perhaps you're just a tenant at your brokerage. What would happen to your existing clients if you couldn't show up because you suddenly had a life event happen? You'd probably get fired, right? More importantly, how about your personal income? What effect would that have if you had to step away for one reason or another?

Think about this for a moment. This is something that happened to a friend of mine. At the time he was making a very good living at sales and had a nice pipeline of business going. He had all the bells and whistles in life. He had a thriving real estate profile (or so he thought). He had an 8,600 square foot home with nine bathrooms, fancy cars and all the typical things money could buy. He really was living life to the fullest. He was in his late twenties when he was suddenly diagnosed with cancer and had to spend over four consecutive months in the hospital. Needless to say, his business went dormant and eventually he lost everything. He realized he had built a business that entirely relied on his presence. It was incredibly demoralizing and once he was out of the hospital, he had to move in to a small room in his parent's home.

The good news is he has since recovered completely and been cancer-free for over 25 years. He has also rebuilt an entire career using the Advanced Agent strategies in his business. He has vowed to never get himself stuck like that again. He started to rebuild his business one client at a time. This time though he understood that he had to build more than just a sales and marketing business. So, he tapped into the residual side of the business to start being productive instead of just busy. He started building a future in real estate he could be absent from and still have money coming in case another life event was to happen. Ask yourself if you know of anybody who has maybe had a life event. Maybe it wasn't as devastating as a serious health scare, but how many people do you know that have been through a divorce or two and had to start over? Life just seems to happen. We all need to be thinking about a long term plan.

If you've ever been excited enough about real estate to go beyond just being busy and wanted to create a real estate business, you could eventually walk away from, you need to start to think about the entrepreneurial side of the business and discover how to be productive instead of just busy. If you care to know more or would like to schedule a discovery call visit: www.MeetupwithRick.com

Making Your Business Work for You, Instead of The Other Way Around

There are many ways to make money in real estate but very few people actually build a real estate business they can walk away from or retire. Do you have what it takes to create a self-sustaining real estate career and keep it working for you? I've been blessed to be one of the few to have achieved this and I'm on a mission to help as many others do the same. What brings me even more excitement and happiness is inspiring and mentoring people to succeed, which is my absolute passion and goal here. Experiencing other people's journey to success, as well as adding value to their lives, is a satisfaction realized greater than most.

I speak to a wide variety of brokers and agents at various stages of their business cycle. Some are just starting out, others have a solid sales history, while others maybe even have a team or independent brokerage. Only a few have really figured it out with enough momentum and true scalability how to maintain cash flow. Even fewer make well into the six and seven figures in their business. Most are so busy they have never even really

While all categories of agents have different challenges in their business, I see common threads among everyone:

- They're working too many hard hours and not spending enough time with their family.
- They're sacrificing their health in lieu of chasing money.
- They are not doing the things they want to do and living their core values.
- They are not making the money they want to make no matter how hard they work or how many hours they put in.

taken score; they just keep grinding and grinding and using **hope** as their solution. I can attest that having a positive mindset is part of success, but that alone will not take you to the finish line. It takes definitive measures. Hope is nothing more than an empty promise.

When I ask people these key questions, the answers are usually the same. The business is not churning as much revenue as they thought because they are so consumed by their daily business. What got them from points A to B does not get them from B to C, and in a lot of cases, hope is the only answer.

Agents, brokers and leaders need to be able to adapt. What I have discovered is that how you achieve your business success is not important. What ***is*** important is that you get there, while living healthy within the boundaries of your core values in spite of just the money.

Consider a Better Way

If you identify with any of these frustrations, you are not the only one who has been saying or at least thinking, "There has got to be a better way" to yourself. I thought it, agents across the country are saying it, and you are right. There *is* a better way.

The Advanced Agent way offers alternatives to running your real estate business **without dramatically changing your existing business model**. Most importantly, it demonstrates how to improve your financial picture. Advanced Agents do this by implementing proven systems and strategies discussed throughout this book. We then guide and support you through the process so that you can run a business which rewards you with more time and money to live the life you choose. Remember, you still have to put in the work; there is no magic formula for success without effort.

Working hard gives us all a sense of pride. But working efficiently can be a lot more rewarding and brings more satisfaction than working simply harder. There are several ways to take your business to six figures and beyond. It's really not that hard when you trade all of your time for money. The issue is that you sacrifice your personal well-being and have no time to enjoy anything. This may make you ask, "Is that really in alignment with the outcomes you desire for your life?"

Wouldn't you rather have a business that produces for you? One that allows your business to work hard for you while creating options on how and where you spend your time? This book will show you how Advanced Agents have made this possible so that you too can create a successful real estate business.

Chapter 1: Take back your time, Stop Laboring & Start Living

The biggest thing I hear from agents and brokers is they have no time to live life on their own terms. It's a constant grind seven days a week, 12-plus hours a day, and they are always reacting to the business. They are typically overwhelmed or just downright frustrated. If you can relate to this, ask yourself who is really in control. Is it you, your business, or your clients? I hear of so many agents becoming a slave to the process.

This business comes with a lot of costs, but they are not just financial in nature. It can have emotional costs too. In fact, many agents bankrupt from the emotional costs before the financial side hits them. The stress of the business carries forward into their everyday happiness. I am sure if you're reading this book, you know exactly what I am referring to. The facts are that there is a lot of liability, financial responsibility and time restrictions. Solo agents and small brokerages try to tackle everything and end up wearing too many hats. This often leads to burnout or just quitting the business entirely. Larger firms have the issue of management and training coupled with high overheads and low margins. Any way you slice it, the struggle is real both emotionally and financially!

The next thing I hear is they have no retirement; most agents work until they die! Why? It's because they have to. There is literally no exit strategy. The Advanced Agent plans ahead for retirement and an exit strategy. Currently, the National Association of Realtors statistics show that the average agent or broker is 53 years old and has zero put away for retirement. If this is you or the path you are headed down, wouldn't it be awesome if you could take back your time and increase your financial well-being while doing so?

Those managing a team of agents always deal with the competencies (good or bad) of the group, consistently spending major amounts of time to keep things running smoothly or paying high costs to managers to handle staff. Instead, they could leverage more profitable systems and others more efficiently to accomplish even more spectacular results.

When analyzing most agents and brokers in the business, we consistently discover most make far less than they anticipated. Maybe you are one of the statistics rated by the National Association of Realtors who averages around $40,000 or less in annual earnings. If we look at the time spent away from what's most important to you, is it really what you desired? Working weekends and being on call constantly connected via email and handcuffed to your phone is even more stressful for most.

The most valuable commodity we all have is *TIME*. How would you feel if you could make more money, build a retirement strategy, offer more value to those around you, and have more free time while doing it? And best of all, you *DON'T* have to change your current business model doing it. Wouldn't that excite you? I know it did me! That's exactly what the advanced agent does. He or she uses the latest in disruptive technology for leads and automating systems of duplication. Then they use leverage of other people's time and efforts responsibly to scale their profits. They build equity while producing sales.

To sum it up, they seek the best of the best. But it must be at the most lucrative levels to scale, gain assets, and build residual income. That currently is only available to Advanced Agents. If you want to be part of this or just find out more on how you too can retire early, gain more freedom and have more money to do what you enjoy most, click right here to discover now or set up a call at www.MeetupwithRick.com or www.Getoffthepaydaytreadmill.com

What Keeps Most Agents from Thriving?

You have probably known agents or perhaps yourself are an agent that works 60 to 80-plus hours a week. You're working every weekend just to sell one property per month. That's a busy agent but not necessarily a productive one. Don't get me wrong; you can make a living from selling one home per month. Let's talk about how to really thrive though.

Agents are notorious for being scattered all over the place because they must wear so many hats. They're also known for being available almost 24/7. They have to keep all of the plates spinning. There is scouting and marketing for leads, making sales calls, receiving client calls, negotiating deals, paperwork, following up on escrows and closings, keeping up with technology, and best of all, being a ringmaster of life both personally and professionally. It's easy to get stretched thin, especially if you are a solo agent. This generates nothing besides exhaustion and agents feeling overwhelmed.

It's no wonder the failure and burnout rates are so high amongst agents, because there are only so many hours in a day and they start sacrificing their personal well-being to succeed professionally. You have to ask yourself if the juice is worth the squeeze. In other words, are you netting the results you want? Also, what's your time worth? What are the other parts of your life you may be sacrificing in order to just stay afloat financially?

Let's step back for a few minutes and work on what you might be able to do differently to help you succeed in all areas of life.

Making Time Work for You

Time is the most valuable commodity we have. Each one of us has the same amount of it - 168 hours per week. You should never sacrifice your health for money. In the end, you'll wind up the wealthiest person in the graveyard. It's critical to get between 44 and 56 hours of sleep a week. This of course helps not only with the body's natural healing process but gives us better cognitive brain power. You should heavily consider spending another 14 hours on personal health goals, namely some form of exercise and self-awareness. This would then leave you around 100 hours per week to split between professional and other personal objectives.

The acronym **DESC** represents how to **D**elegate low payoff activities, **E**liminate distraction, **S**implify your workload, and get results through the proper **C**ommunication. One way to effectively use DESC in your business is to outsource as much low payoff activities as possible. This will give you the highest ROT possible.

Outsourcing, sometimes known as the gig economy and virtual assistants, is a skill or task that can be leveraged by a third party.

Think of it like an accountant or attorney. The idea is you use someone else's highly leveraged skill in the form of delegation. You can also do this very reasonably for administrative delegation too, such as CRM management or social media profile advertising, open house prep, etc. Everything that doesn't immediately put a payment in your pocket at your desired income or hourly rate should eventually be leveraged through delegation. This of course will allow you to focus on your most highly valued personal skills and delegate the ones with low payoff or low reward for you.

A lot of people need more help to grow their businesses. Though sometimes, it can take a few tries to find the right delegation support. The good news is, you just need these three easy steps to manage your life better, become more productive and get the work done easily.

Hire a Qualified VA

List all of the qualities and skills you want your VA to possess. Hire one or more and you can now work on your productive skills. Remember, virtual assistants pull your business forward.

Delegate Your Tasks

After hiring the skilled VA, you can now assign all the low payoff activities and non-income producing tasks that keep you from moving forward. You don't have to do it all by yourself.

Getting the Work Done

It is now time to grow your business. Communicate your desired outcomes. Do the things that you're amazing at and take your freedom back.

In addition to outsourcing, Advanced Agents use systems to help simplify their marketing and workload. In addition, we can share with you how to leverage various strategies to get you to your goals. At the end of the day, there is a wide range of opportunities to take back your time and increase profits. Clarity and accountability are the fast track to obtaining anything worth having. It's simply a matter of understanding **nothing will change until you do**.

Do You Really Value Your Time?

I realize most major roadblocks to jumping towards a higher income tier are due to a couple of things:

- People often spend a significant amount of time, at least 3 plus hours a day, on low-value activities like checking emails, Facebook, texting, and anonymous social rabbit holes.
- Agents spend a lot of time helping people and potential customers or non-clients for free when they could be paid for this effort instead.

While it's not an issue to help others for free and lead with service (which is what I do all the time with friends and strangers), this can be a serious issue for most agents who spend copious amounts of low payoff time each week. Advanced Agents don't mind doing personal favors for others. However, you have to know when to stop and ask for a commitment from your potential clients, and the sooner the better. This is a very competitive and fast-paced business. Because most real estate professionals do give away so much of their time for free, they often wind up feeling unappreciated and drained. How many stories have you lived or heard of your client going with another unrelated agent to procure a transaction? (I thought so.) It's also arguable whether those people actually even appreciated your help as well; most won't even follow up on the help you rendered, much less a thank you.

I will ask you this one simple question: Do you value your time?

Following that, I ask you to join Advanced Agents who are more conscious of how their time is allocated. You will now only pick up clients more in line with your personal and professional goals but you can stop going out of the way to help unworthy clients for free, instead putting that time to better use on clients looking for the value your deliver. You will receive more satisfaction in the end.

Note that it isn't that you have stopped paying it forward; it's just removing the desperation at every request for anyone who contacts you without qualifying them as a valuable use of your time, too.

Advanced Agents become more focused on how to constructively help people's wants and needs while valuing their own time and priorities. It's about realizing that you have tremendous value to give to others and deserve to be paid for the value. Just as how you are happy to pay companies and individuals (like doctors, accountants, and other specialists) for quality services and products.

Focusing on your value will make sure you are compensated properly and it may make you see time as valuable as gold and put it to its highest and best use.

The 80/20 Principle - Your 10K Per Hour

The Advanced Agent does everything in their power to avoid sacrificing their personal life. They take inventory of where and how their time is spent, what their core competencies are, and how to best leverage every moment of their time. It's about maximizing how much an hour of their time is worth and what can be done to increase it.

The 80/20 principle says that if you have 10 rooms in your house, you spend almost all your time in two or three of them. It says if you hire 10 sales people, two of them will generate 80 percent of the sales and the other eight will only generate 20 percent of the sales.

This means that person for person, the two are SIXTEEN TIMES as effective as the other eight. That's right, a good salesperson isn't 50 percent better, he or she is 16X better. That means there's huge leverage in 80/20 principle; it's a lot of momentum to be gained if you pay attention, but much more to lose if you don't.

That means everything in your business is a source of leverage. It means that each aspect has multiple layers of leverage that you can obtain by "zooming in"—$80/20^2$ (64:1) and $80/20^3$ (250:1). It means you can combine many of these factors together and cut huge amounts of waste out of your day and your budgets. This in turn leaves clarity for your focus on the 20 percent maximization.

The 80/20 principle is one of the most fundamental laws of cause and effect. If you're not a math person, stick with me and I'll make this abundantly clear. This is relatively simple and HUGELY important, because if you want to influence buyers—say, sell them a home by putting it up on a billboard—you can accomplish as much with one billboard on a major highway as a thousand billboards on residential streets. That's just a simple, elementary example of leverage. As the story unfolds, you'll discover far more.

You can maximize potential as high as you want until you run out of highways, customers, products, or people. If you have enough series of numbers to run 80/20 five times (to the 5th power), your winners are 4,000 times better than your losers. That's million-to-one leverage and it's not a joke. It's reality.

The 80/20 rule to the 5th power

$80/20^1$ = 16:1

$80/20^2$ = 64:1

$80/20^3$ = 250:1

$80/20^4$ = 1,000:1

$80/20^5$ = 4000:1

Inside every top 20% is another top 20%.

One way to determine if you are spending your time efficiently is to take score. If you earned a $100,000 per year, this means your hourly rate is $50/hour. Therefore, if you perform a $15/hour activity, you're instantly robbing yourself of $35 dollars. That is determined by taking the average of a 50-week work year (with two weeks of vacation) and a 40-hour work week, eight hours per day, at just five days a week.

50 weeks x 40 hrs./week = 2,000 hours, then $100,000 / 2,000hrs = $50.00 per hour

Think about where your last few deals came from. Think about what specific actions it took to generate the deals and nurture them to a close. It's the same 80/20 principle explained above. You'll find that 100% of your revenue came from 20% of your efforts or literal time spent specifically on just those deals. Most likely 80% of your production was generated from just 20% of your efforts on those transactions and produce 100% of your income.

VISIT:

IF YOU WANT TO DETERMINE YOUR TRUE NET WORTH PER HOUR?

TAKE MY WEALTH AGE AND FITNESS TEST AT: WWW.REALWEALTHWHISPERER.COM ON THE HOME PAGE.

IT'S A SHORT EIGHT-MINUTE TEST.

THIS WILL REALLY BREAK IT DOWN TO SHOW HOW MUCH YOU'RE WORTH AN HOUR.

WWW.REALWEALTHWHISPERER.COM

In fact, the broader you look at your income, the more you'll see this to be true. This means if you looked at say the last three years, you'll find that 100% of your income came from just a small portion of actual dedicated time to produce that income. The rest was just busywork surrounded throughout the rest of the time. These are tasks you probably could have delegated or outsourced, leaving you time to focus on your core competencies.

The 10K an hour theory is just that. It's however much money you generated last year or whatever period you'd like to survey. You want to always be working towards making 10K per hour so you can afford to delegate all low payoff obligations. I know this may sound extreme or difficult, but the reality is you are already doing it at whatever value you've accumulated. Now it is to just focus as much of your efforts on doing your highest and best paying activities.

Getting to Your 10K Per Hour Work

There is a lot more $10/hour work in your day than there is $10,000/hour work. These are things like running errands, going to the grocery store, and mundane tasks. Optimizing your database and scaling it, surely that is $1,000/hour work. Closing transactions and negotiating great deals is easily $10,000/hour work, especially if you are an investor or volume producer.

You have to realize that most work throughout your week is going to be low-level activities. The way we know this is true is because if you look back at your last year, I can promise you the majority of your income (the highest 20%) was derived from less than a week or so of actual cumulative work.

What this means is that if you made $100,000 last year, those earnings were produced from only 40 to 80 hours of cumulative work to produce that outcome. The rest of the time was spent on producing low-level income tasks that you must delegate. This is the best way to scale to the highest level.

The reality is whatever you did during those 80 or fewer hours produced that $100,000 income; that time spent creating that money has a higher $10,000 an hour value per hour than all the other stuff that you did throughout the remaining part of the year combined. Let's review some tasks while you gauge where your 10K hour fits best.

You'll discover each sample item proves the 80/20 is true of almost anything you can measure in a business is relevant: review the list below

- Sources of incoming clients and calls (ex. 100 calls = 20 warm leads)
- Sources of online and web traffic (20% of your marketing delivers 80%)
- Effectiveness of salespeople/processes (20% of staff drive 80% of sales)
- Converting leads to clients (only 20% of your leads will become clients)

- Popularity of geographic farms (80% of sales will come from niche popular areas)
- Types of product, i.e. SFR, Multi Unit, Commercial (80% of sales will be in one type)
- Problem employees (20% of empl./agents will cause 80% of your stress)
- Customer service/relations management (etc, etc, etc)
- Sources of conflict (etc, etc, etc)
- Performance of escrow affiliates and lender partners
- Advertising waste
- Advertising effectiveness
- Productivity of web pages
- Activity patterns in a 24-hour day, a week, or a month
- Reasons customers buy

80/20... it's not just true once. It's true over and over again in each benchmark of your business to get to 10K per hour leverage. Each item above has a 20% inside of each 20%.

I remember scrimping and saving on everything when I started my business. I would do everything myself if I could, from graphic designing, to marketing, to all forms of administrative work. I held off outsourcing for a long time because my philosophy was, "Why pay someone when I can do it all myself for free?"

But I realized that I was utilizing a lot of time, usually hours on end, on tasks like troubleshooting tech issues, doing graphic design, and figuring out how to make my entire business integrate. This cumbersome load prevented me from getting to the higher-value tasks in my business; like client retention, branding, and asset development. The low payoff tasks would also cause me to work late until wee hours of the night, because:

1. I'm not an expert in everything, hence I would need to put in extra time to learn the ropes and do the work.
2. The act of having to do something that I was neither an expert in nor enjoyed made the process very draining.

By outsourcing or delegating the low-value tasks, I was able to multiply profits. For example, thanks to outsourcing portals and globalization, it is possible to get good quality help online today starting at very reasonable hourly rates. Yet, I held off from outsourcing because I wanted to save money. I locked myself in with an illogical need to save money — even when I wasn't in a shortage of cash in my business — with the blind objective "to save money." The result was thousands of hours wasted, thousands of hours which could have been better invested in my business to further grow it and earn more income sooner.

Now think about what is your 10k per hour. What are your core talent competencies (strengths)? Focus solely on what you do better than anyone else. What if you could do more of your high payoff activities and delegate the low payoff activities to increase 16% to 64% or even 4,000% of what you're good at? If you just took this one bit of advice, you will be able to take back your time and maximize your profits.

CASE STUDY

Juan and Bettina S.

Juan and Bettina had developed a strong sales business that produced over 80 units per year. Always ambitious and looking to advance their business, they set a goal to sell 125 units per annum but struggled to maintain a work-life balance with their two homeschooled children.

At one point, they realized they faced the law of diminishing returns, which meant that the level of profits or benefits gained was less than the amount of money or energy invested. Their net income for selling 100 units was actually less than selling 80 because of the extra financial commitment of advertising and time commitments they required to make it work.

We arranged a strategy session to step back and apply the DESC approach. What we came up with initially sounded counterintuitive. However, we actually found that selling fewer homes and placing focus and effort on high leverage activities (HLAs) would reap higher returns on their time.

Adding to their business model, we altered their sole focus of working just with sellers and buyers and were able to expand their income streams by also working with other agents. They now experience a healthier lifestyle without sacrificing their overall net income.

Although they have now chosen to scale back their sales to about 40 homes per year, they net the same as they did when they sold 80 units. Juan and Bettina chose to be more selective with the type of clients they work with, refocused on looking at investment deals to add to their personal investment portfolio, and in doing so, have increased their net worth by $300,000 in just two years. With all the additional time they have created for themselves, they now enjoy travelling to new places in their RV, as a family.

**Call to Action----> To learn more about how to take back your time while still increasing profits feel free to connect with me.
Visit: www.MeetupwithRick.com**

Chapter 2: **Predictably Grow & Scale Your Business**

I think we learn best when we model the strategies and behaviors of successful people. Hence, the heart of this book is based on what top level agents and brokers are doing to scale their businesses. To build STABLE income, you need absolutely clear strategies, proven systems, and predictable growth.

Scaling your business to the next level is a milestone for everyone. It's that epiphany when you have complete validation and you realize you want to take your business to the next level, no matter what level you are at today. The problem is the traditional model of real estate is hard to scale for growth. It takes lots of capital, time, and effort. It is a constant grind to search for leads, more clients, and not to mention if you're a broker managing agents and getting the deals to actually cross the finish line.

Sometimes all of this can feel like managing an adult daycare.

Did you know that nationally an average of 37% of all real estate transactions fall out of escrow for one reason or another? Failed transactions can have any number of causes: The bank may find an issue with the buyer's financial history, the home may not appraise for the agreed-upon sale price, or the home inspection may reveal underlying issues the buyer isn't willing or able to take on. Perhaps you have experienced a deal or six that you thought was a sure thing only to get the call last-minute something went wrong. Oops, time to reset. Start over with a new deal, a new buyer and pray for closing.

Perhaps you have a team of agents that constantly require the bulk of your day. Sure you're making a split on them, but how much are you really making in exchange for your time? How much of your own sales production have you had to sacrifice to manage your team?

The main issue we all face is that we only have so much available bandwidth. On top of that, we are only as good as our last transaction. Whether you are a broker or the single agent, it is always a game of cat and mouse; the chase goes on and on. It's a never-ending cycle. The moment we stop selling is when we go into overtime or grind mode to find our next deal. If we are lucky, we have a pipeline of deals or a team of agents working for us. However, it seems the best agents always seem to move on to bigger and better splits or offerings. Agents never seem to show loyalty, let alone gratitude for all the wisdom you bring to the table. Keeping good talent is another consistent grind. Let's face it; it's every agent for him or herself out there.

What if I could share with you a way to eliminate some of these problems in your business or at least reduce your stress levels by sharing a few ways I have created a team of Advanced Agents who are crushing it.

- Would you be interested in unlimited and unrestricted geographic agent/team growth?
- Would you be interested in cutting your overhead from day one?
- Would you be interested if I told you could do this with no agent liability for yourself even as a broker?
- What if I could show you a way to leverage other agents across the nation and keep them working for you?
- What if I could give you full access to top producer training that you and your teams could access from anywhere you have an internet connection?

- What if I could assist your IT struggles and all your Admin details, like accounting, TC's, Training, Broker Liability, etc.?

Oh yeah, and cut your light bill at least in half. Would you think I've lost my mind or would you say this sounds exciting and have to see what this is all about? I hope you have chosen the latter, because what I am about to share with you was shared with me, and I couldn't wait to get started.

The Advanced Agent is all about seeing an opportunity and scaling your business with the latest trends and technology available. It's about mimicking success of the agents who have already mastered these systems. It's about using disruptive technology alongside strategic implementation of all the shifts happening in our industry. In short, nobody wants to be holding the keys to a Blockbuster store when they could be holding the speed and scalability of Netflix.

Using Technology to Scale Your Business Faster

The home office has always been the predominant place of workspace for the most successful industry leaders. Now more than ever, leaders of the industry are leaning toward home and cloud based solutions for ease of accessibility. It also eliminates geographic restrictions, overhead, and time constraints. Therefore, embracing the home office is a natural place of opportunity to cut costs and scale your business.

As expenses rise all around, more efficient processes will overtake our industries. Think about it. What actions are performed by physical brick and mortar offices? When is the last time you closed a transaction in which your client physically visited a real estate office? How about the mortgage lender? I mean, it's a rarity. Almost all of these are done virtually now. Very few if any aspects of closing real estate transactions have the necessity to visit a physical brick and mortar office.

The client or agent simply interacts via cloud based email servers, e-signed documents, scanned files, and mobile notaries. As agents, we also leverage the internet with online courses for standards of training, continuing education courses, and top notch trainers without having to get off the couch. Most agents and brokers are so inundated in their day-to-day grind that all they think about is the "tasks" of their business, NOT how they can grow and scale it. They end up working *in* the business and not *on* the business.

At the end of the day, we all have to remind ourselves that we are ultimately responsible for everything, good or bad. I keep a sign on my desk that says: "OWN YOUR OWN LUCK" to help me remember this. In fact, I trademarked it at the U.S. Patent Office.

But the most successful agents and brokers consistently focus on the ways to exponentially grow their business beyond the day-to-day tasks. They look beyond just lateral modes of growth. Let's look at a couple of ways to scale.

Agents and brokers can only do so much before burning out. You may know what to do and how to succeed in working with buyers and sellers, but do you know how to scale and duplicate this success for continued growth?

Maybe you're an agent looking to grow from 10 deals per year to 20, a $100 Million producer looking to sell over $100 Million, or a broker with 15 agents looking to grow to 100 agents. No matter what growth looks like for you and no matter what challenges you face, everyone is searching for the same results: "How do I predictably grow and scale my business so that I can make more money, work less, and feel great about it?" Consider the flowing.

Scaling Strategy One: How adding team members could help you duplicate your business

This is one of the fastest ways to duplicate your efforts. Imagine if you could clone yourself or at least what you do. I've had both failure and success in outsourcing the vast majority of the "tasks" in real estate – mostly success. However, like any potential team employee or independent worker, vetting them with references is a must. Finding good people can be the toughest job of all; as the leader you have to be fair but firm.

I outsource all of the day-to-day tasks and focus on client follow up and working with lenders, since that is the part that takes one-on-one consultation. Tasks like lead sourcing and scheduling can all be done very successfully by an ISA or VA.

You'll want start by building up your sales and marketing team first, then starting with scaling up your operational or administration team. You need to lead with sales growth to drive the scaling process. Using technology and VAs will allow you to duplicate your efforts in finding more buyers and sellers very successfully.

Scaling Strategy Two: Leveraging technology

How can you use technology in a way to both lower your real costs and achieve scalability? Companies like Zillow, Trulia, OfferPad and other recent direct-to-consumer related companies are all trying to create a more direct peer-to-peer experience, essentially cutting out the real estate agent. The most successful agents and brokers embrace change early on, so they can be cutting edge, while others lag and get left behind.

I know how change was for me; I dreaded thinking about having to make changes in my model. Right away, I knew if I didn't do something to keep up with the shifts in real estate, I would soon become like Blockbuster – relevant but broke!

Implementing a website that has IDX and a preemptive CRM that sends automated follow-up campaigns to your clients is a great way to scale by use of technology. Having systems working behind the scenes is an awesome way to keep in sync with tasks. You can run ads and marketing for certain segments of your business and direct your potential clients through a process of CTAs (calls to action). The right platform for marketing can easily compound your business. In fact, this is how most professionals begin to scale.

These platforms do have a cost and typically recur on a monthly basis. However, if you look at the real cost, you should be making money monthly from your advertising efforts. So, in reality you are actually scaling and making an ROI on your marketing expenses.

We all run our book of business differently. When you develop a system that works for you, that's when you focus on duplication. By creating an overall plan that is clear for your business, you're able to work on predictably scaling your growth.

If you have any questions on how to implement these strategies, reach out to me. Let's set up a strategy session. If you have grown and scaled a real estate company and think I have left something out, I ask you to do me a favor and share it with me on a call together. Visit: www.MeetupwithRick.com to schedule a connection.

Dependent vs. Independent Contractor Scalability

Regardless of your capacity to earn money, the majority of those in real estate can be categorized as either a dependent or an independent contractor. The dependent real estate contractor is not much different than an employee, except without the benefits. They've been convinced that they are dependent on their company brand and brokerage resources to succeed, even though the evidence proves differently. They feel as if they couldn't succeed without the entitlement of their brokerage.

Truth be told, several studies by the National Association of Realtors (NAR) prove that the reason clients chose the agent they worked with had very little or nothing to do with the name of a specific brokerage. In fact, the studies show on average this is only a factor for 3 - 5% of the buyer's and seller's decision to work together. That means the main reason 95% of people choose a specific agent to work with is because that agent personally added value, personal service, and could be trusted. Advanced Agents realize this early on and take full advantage of personal branding strategies.

But don't take my word for it. Ask your previous clients which brand brokerage offers them the most value and benefits. Ask them to be specific about which brand they thought had the most value. Their silence will speak for itself and they will most likely respond, "I chose to work with you as my agent because of YOU." Your personal branding is your most prized asset.

If you feel your personal brand is your best asset to offer your clients, it seems you can identify more with the independent contractor rather than the dependent one. Advanced Agents and I resonate with you. Independent contractors are usually more confident, entrepreneurial, and resourceful, with a "Let's make this happen" or "I'll figure it out" mentality.

Notice how I didn't say experienced. Any agent can become an independent type; it just takes the right vision and confidence. These personality types are the "business builders." They are serious about building their own future instead of somebody else's. They know their strengths and delegate their weaknesses because they've maxed out on what they can do alone. Their hope is to duplicate their success through scaling and bringing others in where their weaknesses are evident.

More Ideas to Scale for Success

Independence is the right thought process in order to achieve success. Keep in mind that there are many ways to build and scale a business. In most cases involving real estate, scaling your business will initially cut into your own production. You'll be investing in other agents' success through training, tools, and systems.

It's important to remember that you eventually want to build a business that won't depend on your presence. You're already experiencing it the other way around, so now it's time to fix that. The vision is to create profits that continue whether you are in the room or not.

One problem with investing time and relying on others is that when your agents find success, they start asking themselves the same questions of how to build a predictable, growing, and scalable business. Soon, they venture off on their own after you've invested in their success, leaving you back at square one. Turnover rates on teams and brokerages of 40% are not uncommon. When this happens, you don't end up with the predictable and scalable business model. I'll share with you how to keep agents with loyalty in chapter 7.

Consider This: Interdependence

The limitation of the dependent and independent agent models is largely due to the fact that they reflect the old top-down "factory type" real estate business models originating from over 20 years ago.

Think about how brokerages typically operate. Where and how are company dollars dispersed? It goes to the owners and brokers who have to pay all of the expenses including rent, training, administrative staff, and other overhead. If you participate with a national franchise model, your regional owners get a piece, as well as the national company. These are costs in the form of monthly franchise fees, royalty fees, or desk fees. As you can see, this is clearly a top-down model where the agents doing the majority of the sales receive whatever is left over.

Here are some honest questions to ask yourself:

- How is the company I produce for reinvesting profits to benefit my future?
- What real value do they provide in return to maximize your real estate business?
- Is this the only way I can succeed? And do they have my best interest at heart?

There Has to be a Better Way! Luckily for You, There Is.

Advanced Agents seek to leverage technology and tools to excel business models that encourage interdependence which promotes an agent-centric model rather than a broker-centric model. The internet has become the great equalizer to our industry by providing more value to customers immediately. This effectively helps streamline information for both the agent and client to work directly together. But more effectively, it eliminates the need for added expenses and overhead costs often found in the older broker-centric, top-down model.

Structuring your business to properly leverage technology allows the creation of true alliances, partnerships, systems, and tools to be seamlessly integrated with competent and trustworthy collaborative members. In short, you have the ability to take control of your future profits and work with the proven strategies that have true modes of scalability and duplication. This generation of real estate professionals will be driven by technology and a tech-enabled agent who participates in it.

It has already happened in other industries, and now it's happening in real estate. Uber, Airbnb and Amazon to name just a few, have leveraged internet technology to create a massive shift using systematic platforms to scale businesses that disrupt the top heavy, top-down, expensive models. Additionally, these companies share the cost savings in the form of discounts to consumers. It's all about how we can connect a more peer-to-peer experience. The world is becoming more interdependent every day.

This is right on track with what Advanced Agents do by streamlining processes and leveraging technology to reduce friction in their workload, resulting in more net time while also reducing overhead costs of production to maximize profits. Take a look at the case study below.

CASE STUDY

The Top Producer - Gene F.

Gene was a top producer. He, like a lot of veterans in the business, had maximized his potential in many ways, or at least he thought so (more in a moment). Over a decade, he had assembled a business consisting of six franchises, a whole host of top agents, as well as becoming an owner of an entire region in Northern California. He had grown and scaled a business model in one of the most traditional ways, over many years, with a lot of hard work and capital intensive.

He had a variable income stream based on the production of his agents and teams. He had a book of business but the issue he faced was that there was no real predictability. He also was responsible for a fixed set of monthly hard costs and overhead. There was a host of liability issues and concerns, with only one way to scale even higher. That way was to add more agents or buy additional franchises, both of which would add to the bottom line but would come with another fix set of costs and liability as well.

When he dove deeper into his business, he started noticing a trend of his top producing agents. They no longer used his offices as much as they used to. When he inquired in mandatory staff meetings as to why they didn't come into the offices, their overwhelming response was "Gene, we don't come in because the offices aren't where the buyer's and seller's clients are." They understood clients leveraged the internet for inventory and connecting with agents that way.

Gene realized that the office was not a major benefit to producing agents as it used to be. In the past, agents used the office to visit with clients to flip through a book of listings. Today, clients go online to research real estate and agents market themselves better than the broker-owners can. Gene understood his business model wasn't predictably scalable or duplicable for him or his agents.

Finally, he arrived at a point where he had to make a choice: either sell everything for what the market would bear or find a better way to advance in the industry.

What he discovered was eye opening. He discovered the way shifts happening in industries like Uber and Netflix were about to disrupt the entire real estate models of doing business as well. The old-fashioned way was going to be outpaced by technology. Disruptors that had outpaced brick and mortar and big box stores like Blockbuster were being introduced in every model of business, including real estate.

Scaling anywhere in the country is now quicker and easier than ever before because the geographically restricted office model has been eliminated and the value proposition that was there to attract the top producers. This led to more available funds to leverage tech-based solutions for agent training, lead generation, transaction coordination, and managing deal flow.

So you can imagine if a veteran like Gene was about to make a move in to the Advanced Agent way of doing business, it just might be worth a further look. Gene ended up selling all of his franchises and dove headfirst into the more profitable way from day one. He had eliminated fixed overhead costs using a cloud-based solution and tying it with technology. He was able to scale more quickly while building more personal profitability. He leveraged the model using tech-based solutions for agent training, lead generation, transaction coordination, and managing deal flow using systems, technology, and the internet to host all of his sources.

Gene now has developed net profit far beyond expectation using the same exact systems as the Advanced Agent literally in a fraction of the time it took him to build an entire portfolio of franchises. He NO LONGER supports over a million dollars in fixed overhead and has more time to spend doing the most important things he chooses.

Call to Action----> If you want to learn how to scale your real estate business in a sustainable way to create a lasting income. To discover how the Advanced Agent benefits and exactly how Gene did it,
visit this link. www.meetupwithrick.com

Chapter 3: Improve Sales, Gain Net Worth, and Create Passive Income

Then vs. Now Sales

How and where did the top-down overhead-heavy business models actually come from? It all started during the Industrial Age when thinking was done at the top and employees executed effective and efficient tasks and operations in the factory.

For over half a century it was expensive to market and provide services; the factory mentality meant only those agents and owners with means could remain profitable. Brokerages needed shelf space and offices, creating a major barrier to entry for entrepreneurs. Agents who had a desire to go out on their own faced many obstacles. Attracting clients required big-budget advertising campaigns and a local effort of beating the streets. The top brands used mass media outlets. It was really a game of big branding versus the agents themselves.

Those days are over and today's industries are being turned upside down. Advanced Agents are improving sales and expansion via technology. The internet has changed the way people live, buy, and do business by leveraging technology and media. Now anyone can start a thriving business, ship goods and services almost anywhere across the globe. A peer to peer economy has become the new norm and we are not turning back anytime soon. The internet has become the great equalizer of our time.

Social media, Google, Facebook, and thousands of other internet-based media have reduced the cost of customer acquisition, opening up every industry to connect directly with target markets. The barriers to entry have been broken down, allowing for incredible opportunities to build thriving businesses for anyone who leverages the right resources. All that is necessary is a small number of leadership skills and the ability to tap into the vast amounts of internet technology, tools, and systems available.

The Direct Connection Economy Working for You

We are now in a direct connection economy which is fertile ground for any real estate broker or agent and influencers. Costly and top-heavy, factory-type business models are dying out because many people realize they're working too hard for someone else and would rather work to build their own future for something they believe in.

The top-down business models are not as profitable as they used to be. Massive retail chains and outlet malls are closing down at a record pace because they failed to innovate and adapt to changing times. Companies like Toys "R" Us, Blockbuster and countless others were not able to keep up with the fast-moving customers who connect with their experience via the internet.

Customers and clients are seeking more fast-paced value and insight through the internet, leading them to personal connections and customized services tailored to suit their desires, needs and schedules.

Anyone today has the opportunity to be a success via technology. Reaching more customers and marketing to specific avatars of your business model has never been easier. Everyone can influence the marketing of particular market sector. Millionaires are created by selling products and services by leveraging global platforms and the internet. The world as a whole is shifting to technology, bypassing the old "climb the corporate ladder" model.

The real estate industry is currently in the midst of a major shift. The Advanced Agent recognizes this as an opportunity. All agents and realtors are able to gain access to all the same benefits that brokers and large teams did without the barriers to entry of the past. Improving sales and building a real estate business across borders that removes geographic restrictions is becoming easier by use of technology. The feasibility of expansion and global reach via the internet far exceeds the restrictions of brick and mortar.

Gaining Net Worth & Gauging for Retirement

The majority of agents pay their company too much money, either through large commission splits, monthly junk fees, or just transaction costs, never getting a return on that money. The fact is most agents never even take score of their net profits. Agents generally don' think in the form of long-term benefits such as building wealth. So, where do those company dollars end up? Well first, upper management takes a piece of the pie. Then it pays for overhead, branding, administrative tools, and other line items. However, the money doesn't come back to you; it's a classic top-down, broker-centric model building their future, not yours.

This leaves no wealth building or equity opportunities for the producing agent. Most agents are simply tenants at their brokerage. The monies paid in are never returned in the form of equity or otherwise. Traditional agents build the equity and business of their broker-owner and not for themselves. This is similar to the client/buyer we would often recommend to become a homeowner in lieu of just a tenant.

Shift Number Two: The Mindset of Being a Part Owner

Now I know the game changer I just mentioned in Shift Number One was pretty incredible, but what if I shared another way the Advanced Agent builds wealth through equity? How about if he or she becomes an actual shareholder/owner of the company they produce for and didn't have to change any course of the current business model? That would be pretty awesome right? It's here and the Advanced Agent is being rewarded right now!

Let me shed some light on this. If you have ever rented a home or an office, you were obviously a tenant. There's nothing wrong with that. However, if the choice were yours, you would have probably rather have been building your own equity ownership instead of someone else's, right? You may have even sold homes to first-time buyers coming from the rental market into full-blown ownership. There is something inside all of us that makes us light up when we have pride of ownership.

When you or your client were in the position of renters and then eventually became owners, in both cases there was still a payment going out each month. This consists of the same method of transacting, but your position went from tenant to equitable owner. That is what is significant. It's the same process but with a dramatically different result. You are building your future and not someone else's.

The opportunity of an Advanced Agents is very similar. The model of doing transactions remains exactly the same: simply produce sales just as before. The significant difference here is the Advanced Agent has the ability to become an owner through publicly traded stock awards in the same company for which he or she produces. **It comes down to this: Would you rather be a part owner of the company you produce for through free stock awards or remain a source of equity to the broker you produce for now?** Advanced Agents have the ability to become owners of the company they produce for right from the start of their production and also through building a tribe of referral agents.

You see, the issue with the traditional model has always been a top-down model. That simply means owners and brokers control all the assets, proprietary elements of the business, branding, and determining the splits; therefore, they keep all the profits. This in itself is pretty normal, right? Stick with me and keep reading.

This has been the historical version for years. It only makes sense. The owners of companies reap the rewards of the companies they own. They build their brands and not yours, leaving you with little or most likely no collateral.

What that means for you is you generate leads. You work hard. You close deals and get a commission. Rinse and repeat, end of the story! Simply put, there isn't any reward other than that. There's not much of a value proposition and no exit strategy whatsoever.

This is a huge problem among most agents and even brokers. There are no 401k plans. There are no rewards of stocks. There no retirement parties or pension plans. At the end of the journey there isn't much tangible. Therefore, a typical agent will work until the end, and I think we all know what that means.

I have a question for you. How many stocks has the company, franchise, or team you produce for awarded you in their company stock? The answer I hear 99.99% of time is **"none."** If you are a broker or owner reading this, same question: How many stocks have you passed on to agents who produce for you? Same answer, right? Why is that? It's because most companies don't have the ability to award stock to producing agents. There's just not enough left over at the end of the day. Again, the traditional model is not an agent-centric model.

I'd like to introduce you to the first of its kind Advanced Agent model that will do exactly the opposite. Let me share with you the vision of a bottom-up model. I will share with you how you create a potential exit strategy beginning with your first production sale. I'll share with you how you can become an instant shareholder/owner in the company you produce for from your very first transaction and compounding growth from there. The more you produce, the closer you get to being awarded additional stock ownership in the company. Your potential stock awards increase based on your production. This model is performance based, just how it should be. Contribute more, earn more!

Imagine what kind of mindset shift you might have if you knew that you and all the agents next to you had the same capability. I don't mean just the ones right next to you; I mean thousands of agents being able to rise up. If they too were on a pathway to success, gaining potential stock awards. Think of agents, no matter where they are in the country or even perhaps the world, rising in the same tide as you. You no longer view them as a competitor or possible adversary, but a strategic ally. That is essentially what a bottoms-up model does. It creates a culture of empowered agents working in unity. It creates a tribe.

The mold of the top-down model will be gone forever. Why? Because when you start to think like an owner, you will become the CEO of your destiny. You will start to change how you look at every aspect of your business. You don't just see commissions and splits. Instead, you see that controlling your leads, making more profits, cutting out expenses, and becoming part of a viable way to create an exit strategy through free stock awards is a way for you to increase your worth.

Here is what you do different: Nothing! You just keep doing what you have been for the last however many years. That's it! Holy crap – you start to build equity right here, right now! Again, it's just for producing the same sales as you have been in the past. No matter where you are in your career, your journey starts to see a horizon that has a built-in exit strategy whenever you are ready.

Don't just see your future, become an Advanced Agent! Book a 15-minute discovery call today: www.MeetupwithRick.com or www.theadvancedagent.com

CASE STUDY

Jeff and Amanda W.

Jeff and Amanda had been ranked the #9 Most Successful Team by their local Association of Realtors. The most stunning part of this accolade is their association of realtors is the second largest Association of Realtors in the nation. They spent about $24,000 a year on lead generation tools. Their team sold over 175 homes a year. They were on a 70/30 split and 3% royalties. These were great stats! However, they didn't own one ounce of equity in the company where they ranked so high! They also wanted to scale up business another notch. Having a rank of #9 was good, but not good enough. They wanted to expand home sales and reduce costs on lead generating tools.

Once they were introduced to the Advanced Agent model, we hopped on a strategy call to discuss how to improve their ranks. After some careful consideration, we were able to not only dramatic reduce their costs of lead gen tools, but we also helped them leverage their existing brand. We showed them how to increase net profit, create some equity ownership, and create monthly recurring revenue on top of their sales production.

Within the first 12 months, they saw an increase to 250 home sales, increasing their ranks and recognition. We implemented a plan to expand their team to create more recurring revenue They now have over $6,000 a month in mailbox money in addition to an increase of $50,000 in sales volume.

The best part is the method of doing business is equal, except they have more leverage and accumulated a multiple of stock awards, increasing their net worth and creating a future exit strategy. It was the use of more strategic Advanced Agent methods, models, and structure that enhanced their business. The main day-to-day actions and operations stayed exactly the same.

If you want to know how you can increase your net worth and continue doing the same exact business you've come to know, reach out to me or visit this immediate overview now.

Call to Action----> If you want to learn how to increase sales and start building your own nest egg of wealth and cash flow, get in touch with the me at: MeetupwithRick.com

Chapter 4:
How to Squash Overheads and 10X Your Profits

We all know that it takes money to make money. In addition to money, it takes a lot of emotional capital and hard work to remain relevant in our business. It's either feast or famine. Some months we are crushing it with income, and other months there are barely enough funds to pay for our marketing, coaching, training, and keeping our administrative team paid (and Lord help you if you have an office or two to support and maintain).

If you're like most heavy hitters or brokers, you are always up against all these costs including rent, and technology, not to mention lead-generating platforms, desk fees, and brokerage costs. Whatever it is, the list goes on. Does it ever quit? Let's just say you have a lot of recurring expenses each month that need to be maintained to keep your business running smoothly. For me, I knew that if I tried to cut expenses, I would most likely lose momentum in sales. I had to always struggle and keep my pipeline as full as possible. After all, that's the name of the game, right? Always be selling, marketing, and closing!

When I asked Whit Garret, a 37-year broker in the industry, what he thought his net profit was, this is what he had to say about being a broker: "Gross profit is all the money a company earns. Net profit is what is left after all expenses have been paid. There is not a set rate." Factors like rent, utilities, and average commission vary office to office, state to state, and country to country. It also varies depending on how it's run. If the owner(s) pay themselves salaries, the company may break even or show no profit at all.

Gene Frederick told me that you can only sell your company for about two to three times the net profits, usually in an up-trending market.

I soon started to realize I was no better than any of these guys. I mean, nobody has any magic formula to create more income unless you added more agents, but this of course means more expenses and liability. I knew there had to be something else out there. Then this incredible model (opportunity) was introduced to me. It wasn't until I was introduced to the Advanced Agent way of doing business I became more profitable from day one. Of course, previously, I was making money and sometimes a lot of it, but I wasn't using leverage. I didn't have access to duplication and technology and I wasn't in control of my expenses. I didn't feel like I was gaining personally. I started to wonder who was working for whom – and even more so, why?

To 10X your business, you have to change your mindset and think like a 10Xer. You have to implement the tools that Advanced Agents use to multiply their profits and productivity. Early adoption is one of the best ways of doing business and is key in the modern world. Knowing you can eliminate expenses is actually a profit center for you.

Whether you are new to this business or a seasoned veteran, there are a number of fixed costs that go along with running a real estate business. The most successful agents and brokers actually use other people's time and efforts to scale and leverage. Then they implement systems to scale that leverage. This is the fastest way to increase your monthly revenues. Using this strategy helps to slash your recurring costs. Using proven systems and becoming an early adopter in technology as it unfolds saves a lot of time, too. Those who shift quickly to changing cycles make the most profits. It's always going to come down to the bottom line and cash flow. So, what is your most expensive outlay? Most likely, it's your office expenses followed by administrative costs and lead generation.

If you've ever dreamed of owning a franchise, the lower end can cost near $35,000 for the licensing rights alone. Of course, this is all just the beginning; the actual building, the lights and computers, then insurance and liability on several levels follow.

The solution to this is a highly accessible version called the Advanced Agent. Here lies the way to squash your overhead expenses and continue 10Xing your profits. You start by eliminating expenses like the two I mentioned, your office and administration costs. This goes without saying, but you could possibly even exceed 10Xing your profit from day one, then you implement the systems of duplication. Now, I am sure you are asking how this can be possible. (See the case study below.)

The amazing thing is you'll have a more accessible tech-based solution you can access from anywhere you have internet availability. Most agents already have a home-based solution. You can cut costs of employees and still maintain a co-working space on a temporary basis if you desire, but you'll see over time how that too isn't a necessity. Just by following the Advanced Agent System, it will give you the power to enhance your profits.

Even if you've been looking at other proven ways to 10X your business, can you fill your pipeline and convert sales profitably? What's the next evolution of your career? Maybe it's starting or growing a team, or maybe you're thinking about getting your broker's license, or you want to take this big time and buy a real estate franchise or even start your own independent franchise.

Here are a few other questions you might want to consider as you strategize:

- Have you asked why are you thinking like this?
- Do you know the end game?
- How much capital will it take and when will I see an ROI?
- What's your exit strategy?

- Can you sell out? When and how much would it be worth?
- What do you really want to get out and how long will it take?

Here are a few common growth building principles to consider.

Idea #1 for 10Xing: Build Your Real Estate Team

Building a real estate team is the most common way for strong producers to initially scale without massive up-front financial investment. They initially seem like low overhead models and work well for many big producing teams whose sales volumes are impressive.

However, in most cases, the team leader is also the top producer. The leader of the team usually has to sacrifice personal production. They spend 90% of their time training and oversight of all aspects of operations. Almost all leads and production are dependent on the team leader to make it rain. All of their time is spent training, recruiting, and agent retention efforts dissipate without their presence and dedication.

Advanced Agents have the ability to grow a team of agents without geographic restrictions or the time constraints of personal oversight and training efforts. It's truly a win-win for all Advanced Agents to build a team.

Idea #2 for 10Xing: Create Your Own Independent Brokerage

Starting your own independent brokerage is also an option. All you have to do is create enough value to attract agents to your brand which, oh yeah, costs money. You need tools, systems, an office, and employees – unless you want to be the tech person, transaction coordinator and wear another 15 hats.

You have to take time to educate your agents and provide sales training. You will also need to keep them motivated and accountable. Additionally, you will have to tailor to their needs or they will leave for another brokerage company who offers them more value after they've built up their business on your dime.

Idea #3: Buy a Franchise

Buying a franchise costs money. We're talking about between a $20,000 and $75,000 investment to buy a franchise, franchise fees, royalty fees, and desk fees. In many cases, you don't break even until you have 50+ agents due to all the overhead expenses you will incur.

On the plus side, you do get an entire system and can be up and running in a shorter amount of time than if you go it alone. Going with a franchise brand might help in giving an artificial security to agents. However, studies by the National Association of Realtors have proven it makes very little impact on the client's decision on which individual realtor they choose.

Idea #4: Tapping The Business Like Advanced Agents

Times have changed in the last 20 years. It used to be that brokers brought all the value to the table because they had an office. Clients would walk into a broker's office, sit with an agent to flip through a book of listings, and receive a consultation with one of the broker's agents.

That is no longer the case. Instead, 90% of buyers and sellers go online first to research real estate. Only then do they call an agent they have found online or someone who is referred by their inner circle of relationships.

The real estate transaction experience is now conducted at a peer-to-peer level. Clients use the internet and agents use home offices or shared office spaces like WeWork and Regus, which provide fully furnished and staff supplied offices at a fraction of the cost. The traditional office has dropped way down the list in value as an added benefit for both agents and clients. Now it's all about convenience and speed. We live in times where everybody wants instant gratification.

The Advanced Agent recognizes this as an opportunity. As Warren Buffett says, "Price is what you pay. Value is what you get." By squashing undervalued overhead and reinvesting the savings in high-leverage opportunities to grow their business, Advanced Agents are able to 2X, 3X, or even in some cases. 10X their bottom-line, as in the case study of Terry below.

CASE STUDY
The Broker/Owner Model -Terry Hooker

Terry was a successful agent with Realty Executives and his sales volume exceeded $30 Million per year. He, like most agents, decided he wanted to take his business to the next level. Like most traditional thinking, his next steps were to start his own independent brokerage. He was successful in that endeavor and called it called Axiom Realty. Terry set his sights on recruiting his business to a team of 100 agents. Lo and behold after 17 years of building his business, he had opened three independent office locations with a total of 10 agents.

The leases for his three offices cost him well over $100,000 in reoccurring overhead. He had mediocre technology for his agents to generate leads that cost him over $12,000 per year. He had to hire full-time admins for support and service. On top of all that, he no choice but to sacrifice his own sales production to spend time training and managing his agents.

Terry was burning himself out. He wanted to find a solution to cut his overhead so he could focus more on what was important. His current model was going to eventually implode if he didn't make a change. He sought a way to add growth without additional cost and take back control of his time.

Terry was introduced to the Advanced Agent model and immediately took a liking to it. After watching a quick overview of the benefits, he immediately scheduled a call with us to get started. He saw how he could immediately squash his office overhead and instantly put over $100,000 back into his pocket right away. He also was able to see how it could leverage a more advanced lead generation platform for each of his agents and immediately start building a team of agents who weren't restricted by his location.

The best thing was not only did he increase his bottom line, he was able to increase the value proposition he delivered to his agents. This put him well on his way to his goal of having a team of 100 agents he had been trying to accomplish for seventeen years. We were able to implement an Advanced Agent attraction system where he offered so much more value for all his existing agents and recruits.

In just a short 10 months, he was able to grow from 10 to over 52 agents. That's a 500% growth rate! Wow! And best of all, he did it without sacrificing his brand, that he had been working to build for over seventeen years.

We delivered a lead generation platform to all 50-plus agents and eliminated his $12,000 in previous costs. In addition, by delegating administrative tasks, we showed him how to provide enhanced sales training and better access to support for his agents. Overall, he massively reduced his overhead, he's generating more profitable revenue and now experiences less stress and has way more control over his time.

To get access to exactly how Terry did it, we invite you to schedule a quick discovery call by simply visiting www.MeetupwithRick.com

Chapter 5: Control Your Leads, Control Your Business

The advancement of technology creates a more decentralized economy every day. This is a double-edged sword, depending on how you set your sail to the winds of change.

There are two types of realtors: those of us who already own our business and those of us who want to own our business. One thing about being a realtor is you have the opportunity to control your business even if you work for someone else as an independent contractor. Essentially, you can own your business no matter what by controlling the source of your leads and who gets to manage them.

One of the largest expenses an agent or broker incurs is marketing and lead generation. Then there is the problem of making sure all the platforms you purchase integrate seamlessly. If you are lucky, you can get everything to flow and set up marketing channels on autopilot; this is often not the case. Here is where you hire the IT staff to come to the rescue.

The problem of buying leads from websites like Realtor.com and Zillow is that leads are saturated and super expensive for a possibly low-converting lead. They want the future of real estate to be powered by their technology platforms and exclusive agents. They take full advantage of their dominance by charging agents exorbitant fees to participate. Or, in some cases, these companies seek to circumvent the agent entirely to put more money in their own pocket.

When I started out as an agent, I often wondered who was actually in control of my business. I was surely dependent upon someone else or third parties to keep supplying me leads and a pipeline of business. Of course, I was always having to give up a large share of the split, again not feeling like I was the one owning my career.

Any platform in the market worth having must have a Website IDX (internet data exchange) and an integrated CRM (customer relationship management) system. It has to allow for marketing at the click of a few short steps, just click and paste. These are how you stay consistent in marketing. The most successful platforms on the market easily run $600 to $1,500 per month and the typical firm ends up paying huge expenses for platforms like this. It just becomes a cost of doing business. The other issue is these costs never go away, even in the bad times.

Here's another thing to think about. Whoever is managing the leads gets to cherry pick the good stuff, and if there's anything left, they throw a bone to the agents below them. Again, it's feast or famine. Too many agents are spread too thin over the same number of leads. Of course, this only makes sense, right? The person on top paying the expenses should yield the benefits, right? Wrong!

The problem with that is you are never building your own book of business. It's always based off someone else's strategy and control. They feed you what they want and not what you deserve. You put in the time and then split your commissions for your hard work.

I finally realized that I was being leveraged. My efforts yielded someone else a piece of my earnings.

It wasn't until I became an Advanced Agent with a company that gave me a full control of my book of business that I really gained momentum. Once I had my own independent platform to control my inbound leads and outbound marketing 100%, I could log in and start to own my own business. I was now in control and responsible for creating my own leads, which meant I was the one who managed them. I could do and market whatever I wanted to my database. I could set up my own drip campaigns and take back my efforts and reward myself for my time spent nurturing clients.

Once you have the technology platforms in your hands, this dominates a huge shift in your career. From that point forward, no matter where I went or who I worked for, my book of business was mine to keep. I always knew I wouldn't be starting from scratch; no matter where I moved, my database went with me. This is a shift from a lead-dependent agent to an abled-tech agent. Your database is your key to unlocking growth.

Is Technology Driving Real Estate Agents Extinct?

The good news is that buyers' and sellers' use of an agent remains at historical highs -- 87% and 89% respectively. FSBOs remain at an all-time low of 8% in the U.S. marketplace. Buyers who would use their same agent again or recommend their agent by referral is 89%. On the other hand, 51% of buyers found their home online, with that number rising consistently over the course of the last five years. Only 30% of buyers found their home with the help of an agent.

So the question is whether technology can truly replace the agent. There are arguments to be made in favor of both sides but it really comes down to cost versus value. An Advanced Agent is agile, adapts, and adds value and experience above and beyond what any technology can offer. The overwhelming amount of information and available options actually develops a counterintuitive result for online seekers. Clients are often overwhelmed by the technology options. They seek a more personal, customized service to deliver their desired outcomes.

It's a good rule of thumb to remember your client is in control of the decisions and you as a representative are in control of the process. Most customers don't know the ins and outs across our industry. It takes a professional who can scour through all the clutter and assist with making intelligent and informed decisions. Clients are looking for value, so think of yourself as a concierge and add exceptional value. This is something only two humans can accomplish and find common ground.

Embracing Technology for Survival

The use of technology for an agent is key to their survival. The "no tech agent" days are over. Instead, it's "innovate or lose market share." However, the average agent spent less than $1,600 per year on technology.

To compete in today's tech-enabled real estate market, the best technology tools are expensive and can cost up to $8,000 or more annually. That's not even including the ad spend which can tack on additional thousands for effective marketing campaigns.

You could save money by cultivating and nurturing your sphere of influence (SOI). Your SOI should always be a part of your marketing strategy. Leveraging technology and a good customer relationship management (CRM) platform is vital to expanding your revenue.

The agent that stays top of mind in the lives of their SOI get the deals, and the Advanced Agent leverages technology not just to maximize their consistent and persistent exposure to their SOI to stay top-of-mind, but to advance it daily too. How many physical handshakes can you realistically make weekly within your SOI versus digital handshakes? There is no contest, and when done right, digital handshakes can be automated and become just as effective.

Who's Driving Your Leads?

If leads are being passed down to you from your broker-owner or team lead, the good ones have most likely been cherry picked already and the leads are probably not exclusive. Other agents fight in a rotation to get the breadcrumbs. Doing business this way, you never build your own book of business. It's always based on someone else's strategy and control. They feed you what they want to, rather than what you deserve. You need to be in control of your lead flow if you want deal flow. If you don't control your leads with your own system and setup, you don't control your future.

Of course, you can purchase leads through the internet. However, part of the challenge is the vast amount of technology options out there who all claim to be the best, but at what cost?

There are lots of "vendors" that are more than willing to sell you leads. All you have to do is sign up for several hundreds of dollars per month and off you go. Some provide you two decent leads and others may promise you'll get 200 leads per month. The issue here again is that you're not really in control of driving those lead sources. How did we get to a place where we pay up front before we see results? As agents, we don't get paid until our client's transaction completes, so why should we pay up front before we even know if the technology works as claimed? The various technology integrations and number of combinations that could work requires a full-time tech guru just to figure it out and explain it to you – unless you want to be the guru on top of everything else you're expected to be an expert at.

Providing Your Own Leads

What if you could generate your own leads exclusively and build a stronger personal brand that promotes you? What if you had control over your real estate sales business that included marketing and lead generation? What about your own website? How about having your very own customizable marketing plan and platform integrated with a CRM? Fully automated email campaigns and text capabilities to your entire database? Ad placement at the click of literally a few buttons from your smart phone or computer?

The Advanced Agent leverages technology not just to nurture their sphere of influence but to also capture new leads utilizing systems and tools. They don't chase their clients, waiting for them to be ready to buy or sell. Instead, they let their clients come to them when they're ready. They know exactly when the timing is right and like a genie, the Advanced Agent is there to grant buyers and sellers their real estate wishes.

The Advanced Agent leverages the concept of integrated bolt-on technology systems. Just like a sports team doesn't need the best talent to win the game, they instead need a likeminded synergy and a strategy that can be easily executed.

The Advanced Agent recognizes the changes in the behavior of the customers and economy so that they can shift their position and adapt their strategic business formula. They plan on purpose so that they control the leads coming in. In turn, they become rainmakers in their own right to feed other agents with leads.

By structuring the right partnerships, you can gain access to the top CRM tools and systems and even get your ad spend covered as well. Local, regional, and national partnerships, as well as virtual assistant teams, can massively reduce or even fully cover most of the up-front marketing expenses, allowing you to simply focus on your core competency of sales and closing deals with qualified leads.

It's easy to become burned out by making repetitious calls to discover the diamonds in the rough. That's why the Advanced Agent fully leverages a business model that includes delegating low payoff activities, oftentimes integrating an inside sales agent or team member to scrub the leads. Although there are some intermittent working parts to this structure, it always focuses on the highest and best use of your time. We have been able to guide many traditional agents and help them integrate processes seamlessly through our system.

CASE STUDY

The 10-year Veteran - Alfred A.

Alfred started his career in real estate from the typical journey of an average salesperson. He was always searching for the next source to generate more leads. He hustled for business and worked every angle. He had the typical sources of his sphere of influence, holding open houses, and what he could scab off his broker. Alfred was good at discovering leads on his own. He managed to grind his way to becoming a top producer at his company. The real struggle he faced was this was always a difficult way to scale. He realized that after 10 years of being at his brokerage. The company had provided him lead generation tools that had given him only one qualified lead he could bring to a closed transaction.

He decided to move his license to Berkshire Hathaway, another national brand currently under the helm of billionaire Warren Buffett. He ended up spending $37,000 of his own money and 10 months trying to improve his leads and scale his business. The reason he spent so much money was he was buying saturated leads from Zillow and third-party sources at a very high cost. He started to realize it was the leads he owned in his database, the sphere of influence he had created and controlled that made him the most money. Alfred thought maybe the only way to expand his business would be to start his own brokerage.

It was upon that quest that he discovered the Advanced Agent model. Once he watched the webinar overview, he was blown away on how much more profitable he could become instantly. It was more than us just having the best lead generation tools, it was about having all the tools and strategies Advanced Agents use in scaling business. From owning and master marketing to his very own leads, to moving those leads through a system and closing more deals, the additional profit centers he discovered of Advanced Agents became the icing on the cake. We immediately hopped on a call to discuss the best strategies to implement from day one.

Within his first month of implementing the systems and strategies, he started generating 60 - 100 leads per month FREE with no ad spend. He took control of his own agent dashboard for his CRM, his website, leads, and marketing. He has since grown a team of over six producing agents using the Advanced Agent strategies.

Call to Action----> If you want to learn how to control your leads and grow your book of business at a fraction of a price that most high producing teams do, get in touch to arrange a strategy session at. www.MeetupwithRick.com

Chapter 6: Your Monthly Reoccurring Income Strategy

Question: How many of you reading right now have more MONTH left at the end than the MONEY? If you answered ME to this question, you are not alone! Well this is the GAME CHANGER! Nothing in the business compares to having a monthly residual income. It's the key to financial freedom that moves you from employee to entrepreneur in the cash flow quadrant.

One of the biggest dilemmas in real estate has a common theme throughout this book. It's either feast or famine in all aspects...too many leads or not enough leads. Too many expenses, not enough revenue; a ton of deals all at once or not a damn thing closing. It like a rollercoaster not knowing where the next twist or up or down cycle will end. The real concern is there is NO predictability.

One thing the traditional firms have never figured out is how to potentially compensate the independent agent or broker on a monthly basis – until now! No one has ever been given a system where they could leverage other agents' production and get paid for it no matter where they physically located, and what's better yet, get paid every time that agent closes a transaction – FOR LIFE!

Think of it as a lifetime referral plan. The Advanced Agent has the ability to do just that nationwide. Imagine an agent in your tribe from New York closes a transaction while you're licensed in any other state, like California or Arkansas. Think of it as having your own referral network that pays you from now on every time they close a deal. Now that's leverage – and it's pretty awesome. Most state brokers wish they could do that because not possible in the traditional model.

The common evolution of a typical realtor is to start out as an agent, grow for a few years, and then evolve into a broker or start a team. Perhaps that is where you are now. Then they pay for a franchise or start a boutique brokerage to compete with the big boys on the block. This usually requires getting an adequate office space, appropriate administrative staff, and all the expenses I mentioned in the previous chapters. The next step takes several years to grow out about 50 agents.

Most successful teams and brokers need close to 50 agents for a profitable equilibrium tipping point. They soon discover production sales volume is comprised by about 20% of the agents doing any real business. The other remaining 40 agents only create a host of liability and eat up revenues by bogging down the administrative staff, office space, and insurance premiums.

One of the ways the Advanced Agent creates mailbox money is to put the scalability of a traditional broker model into every single agent's hands starting from day one. How's that for awesome leverage? The best part is you don't have to be a broker to do it. You don't have to be tied to any geographic area, allowing you to expand your team across borders and state lines. In fact, you are free to build a network of agents that can provide you a check in your mailbox every single month and have zero liability for their transactions. Sounds too good to be true, right? Wrong again! It's absolutely possible when working as an Advanced Agent. That's pretty damn cool. Remember, all ships rise in a high tide.

So, let me ask you another question: If you decided to stop selling today or were forced to stop your business due to illness or a life event, what would you have to show for the time you've invested into your career? What would happen to your income? If the answer is that your revenue stops, you are not alone! You are like every other status quo traditional agent in the business.

In addition to not having any revenue coming in, I can with almost all certainty bet the company you produce for is not concerned about your future retirement plans or exit strategy. In fact, keeping you unaware of this downside of an agent's career is in their best interest. Most companies and ownership are dependent on you to keep producing for them to generate revenue. Similar to what I said earlier, you are basically a tenant at their brokerage. You will be viewed as a quasi-employee without the benefits. It's simply you trading your precious time for a commission payment. They offer no other value proposition, no matter how well-known the company or brand.

With all the support and service your company may claim to offer, they generally forget about offering you an exit strategy plan. In fact, they don't forget – they can't! You are completely on your own accord. You're going from hero-to-zero with every single transaction. Let's be real for a minute. If you weren't a profit center for them, you wouldn't be there nor would they exist.

If you have any doubt about this, I dare you to ask your existing company leadership this question: "My goal is to retire in 10 years or less with approximately $7,000 a month in reoccurring residual income. Can you show me the retirement strategies the company offers?" You'll probably get a blank stare, which is equal to, "I don't know, but if you figure it out please let ME know. I'd like to do the same."

The majority of agents are only aware of traditional ways to generate additional income: leave your broker, then evolve into a team or become a broker/owner yourself by paying for a franchise or starting a boutique brokerage. Then, in turn, you repeat the cycle or process and do the same to your agents by keeping them uninformed to keep them producing for you until your top producers fly the nest and become Advanced Agents themselves.

When you join a team of Advanced Agents, you will soon realize how you can get paid on an entire referral network reoccurring each and every month so long as they too are producing real estate sales. It's the ultimate mailbox income strategy. Imagine if you could build a tribe of agents without geographic restrictions (nationwide) and get paid when they do their job. In essence, they close a transaction and you get paid, too.

Every Advanced Agent has the ability to expand a network of agents and/or brokers within their referral business. The amazing thing is like clockwork, the agent that invited them to the group will receive a piece of the transaction when it closes. Best of all, the closing agent gets to keep his or her full earned commission. There is nothing new here to share on how referrals work. In fact, it is very commonplace in our industry. But because you are now part of an Advanced Agent economy, you have the ability to earn a little piece of the pie (closings) from your personally-referred group.

What separates an Advanced Agent from the rest of the agents and brokers out there is that Advanced Agents will be paid not just once, but each and every time on the referred agent's transactions so long as both parties are in good standing with their perspective licensing authority and remain within the network. This also means producing real estate transactions in their typical course of business.

Advanced Agents can compound their monthly income by expanding their agent count, similar to a broker expansion model except without the liability and without geographic restrictions. This allows every single agent from day one to scale their monthly passive income without the stress of being a broker. There is no massive overhead which allows you to expand across borders and state lines immediately. It's all done based on relationships that have and create. You have the freedom to build a tribe of agents that can put a monthly check in your mailbox over and over again. Best of all they (your tribe) can too!

Call to Action----> If you want to learn how to generate these mutually beneficial relationships with your agents or brokers, get in touch to arrange a strategy call with us. www.MeetupwithRick.com or visit www.getoffthepaydaytreadmill.com

The Cashflow Quadrant Mindset

Advanced Agents not only have all the strategies described so far, but most importantly, they have a long-term mindset and understand the Cashflow Quadrant taught by **Robert Kiyosaki** in his book **Rich Dad Poor Dad**. If you haven't read it, I highly suggest you add that to your list of must-reads.

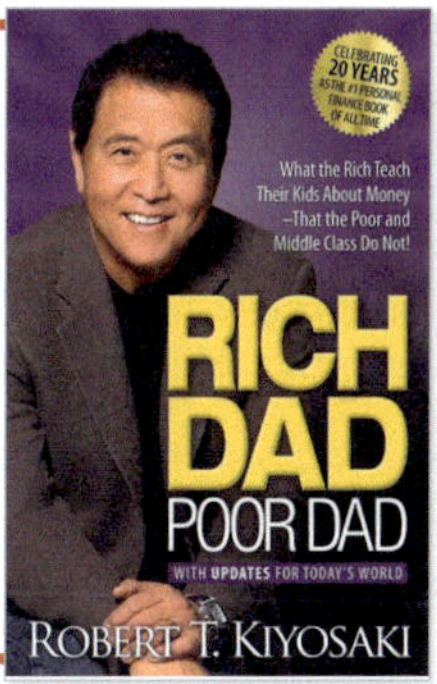

Mr. Kiyosaki had two fathers growing up, a poor dad and a rich dad. He explains how his rich dad taught him how to become financially independent using the Cashflow Quadrant.

I encourage you to review the quadrant and if you have any questions, I'd be happy to address them personally in our strategy call session.

Advanced Agents know they can't sell forever. Early in their career, they strategize on how to develop passive income via the Investor Quadrant shown in the graphic. The sooner you get your money working for you the better, and the sooner you start to focus on your 10K an hour productivity, the better. Finally, if you can shift your focus along the way to business models that develop recurring income, you will have a rewarding career and at least a plan for retirement instead of just relying on hope!

Our Advanced Agents are focused on various strategies for building assets for their future and monthly reoccurring cash flow through leverage. This is true passive income.

CASE STUDY

$4K and Beyond in Monthly Mailbox Money- Mickey C.

When Mickey was first introduced to us, he wasn't the typical sales agent. He hadn't become a broker yet, but he was part of a high producing team. The real issue was he was only as good as his last closed transaction, despite the high volume. He was looking for ways to create some predictable monthly cash flow. At the time, he worked for a traditional well-known brokerage. His production consisted of above-average sales per month. The biggest problem was that he was consumed by trying to keep those deals closing and tracking progress. The team split ratios were also greatly weighing on his bottom line income.

We introduced him to the Advanced Agent model. This really opened his eyes to the possibilities of having true residual income for himself. Within six months of adopting a strategic business plan, Mickey now regularly earns over $4,000 in monthly recurring income from a small networking team of his own agents. He is not stopping here.

By the same time next year, he will have most likely doubled his mailbox earnings potential through our compounding growth model. This means he has the ability to earn income on the agents his agents bring in. The best thing out of all this is this reoccurring money is in addition to his own production. He now has a group of referral agents he can count on for recurring revenue each month. Everyone who becomes an Advanced Agent has the ability do the same thing as Mickey right from the beginning.

Our model has changed the way teams, team leaders, agents, and brokers are able to earn more income beyond just their own production. We are able to share with you the potential to be paid on an entire referral network for every transaction for life from day one.

You don't have to be tied to any geographic area. You can be licensed in any state and grow in another. This allows you to expand your agents across borders and state lines at a fraction of the cost. In fact, you are free to build a tribe of agents that can provide you with a check in your mailbox every single month and eliminate your broker liability of those agents simultaneously. Our model is the fastest way to put the broker growth model into the palm of every single agent on the planet regardless if you started in the business yesterday. This immediately goes beyond your own sales. It is additional mailbox money that comes every month whether you personally have sales closing or not.

To learn more visit: www.getoffthepaydaytreadmill.com or schedule an immediate call @ www.MeetupwithRick.com

Chapter 7
The Agent Retention Model: Give Them the Biggest, Most Lucrative Reason to Stay

The cost of agent turnover is high. It takes a lot of commitment, time, and financial investment to attract the right agents to your business in the first place. If they're not already producing, then it's a matter of training them to succeed and keeping them productive. Expecting agents to stay with you just because of your ego or brand puts your priorities ahead of theirs – it's naive and quite self-centered.

Offer Agents Ownership

So, what's the best agent retention model? It's simple: Give them the most lucrative reason to stay by offering them ownership in the business and share a portion of the revenue with them.

When you own something, you treat it differently. You take care of it because you have that pride of ownership. When you recognize and reward agents financially for helping you to grow your business, you've not only given them a valid reason to stay, but a lucrative one too! The reason most agents aren't loyal to any one brokerage or company is there is no incentive to stay beyond narrowing the commission splits.

OFFER AGENTS OWNER SHIP

Advanced Agents are able create an environment for themselves to become owners in their company no matter if you just started in the business a week ago. There a few ways they are able to do this. I want to be clear in stating that any agent – young, old, new, or experienced veteran – has the ability as an Advanced Agent to participate from day one. Everybody is on the same playing field when it comes to potential stock awards. Notice I mentioned awards. That means for you just making certain benchmarks of performance as you would at any brokerage or company, you will receive publicly traded stock for hitting those benchmarks – for free! Yes, free!

Personally, I'm very selective about the people on which I invest my time and resources. When the main focus is price and cost rather than value, it's a major red flag. It's a scarcity versus abundance mentality. Of course, price and costs are important to manage, but let's focus on the $1,000 you'll make rather than dwell on the $100 here and there that you might incur in expenses. It's all about focusing on short-term returns, yet long-term value. I have experienced agents who tell me they're on a 100% commission structure. When we analyze their net earnings after fees, it is common to see well over $20,000 paid into their brokerages for relative fees. So, I ask you if is that truly100%.

Think of it like this. A net seller's statement focuses on what the client will net after all said costs and expenses. What remains is the NET. Well, there is no difference in our business models at the end of the month or year; it's about how much we kept NET versus our commission split. Advanced Agents often realize net yields over 100% commission due to stock awards and monthly passive income.

So what type of agent are you? What type of agents do you want to be associated with in your business? Agents that make decisions based solely on price or those that understand value is what you receive and price is merely the conduit to receive that value.

The Advanced Agent doesn't ask what the split or price is. Rather, a savvier question I hear from Advanced Agents is, "How much earning potential do I have and what am I getting in value?"

The value proposition is shifting. The agent's ability to market themselves, leveraging lead generation technology and social media, allows the agent to reverse the role brokers or owners have with what value they bring to the table. Only interdependent Advanced Agents think like this.

This creates a dilemma for broker-owners, team leaders, or anyone looking to scale their business by attracting the top producers to work with them. Loyalty is a valuable character trait but let's be real. If an agent can significantly grow their business and career and improve the financial well-being of their family, loyalty goes out the window. It would be financially irresponsible for an agent to not consider a better financial opportunity.

We all know the best agents are always seeking the best opportunities in the business. This again only makes sense. I mean, why wouldn't they? The best talent comes and goes, so the one biggest challenge is keeping your A-Team list of agents and scaling sales volume.

But what if you could turn that around? What if there was a system in place to make agents want to stay on their own free will. Wouldn't it be cool if you had a value proposition that encouraged your agents to stay for the long term because they received benefits beyond just what every other competitor offers?

Well, that day has come! The most lucrative reason agents stay is they are offered unparalleled value, more access to scale their own business, and a way to become vested through ownership in the company they go out and hustle for. Never before has an agent been able to become an owner in a nationwide, publicly traded brokerage. The Advanced Agent has that offered to them from day one with the ability to be awarded stock for producing sales just like before. Except now not only do they earn just a commission, but working towards stock awards, too.

Imagine if every year you closed your first deal, you received a piece of the pie of the company just for closing that deal. Boom, automatic stock award! It's the same model of business as before, except now you are a vested owner. Pretty cool, right?! Imagine if you capped your split with the same company and they gave you more public stock in that company.

Wouldn't that change your earnings and attitude? The number one thing that tribes admire is having a sense of belonging to something bigger than themselves.

Even if you are a solo agent now and even if you don't see a future of agents working for you, you can still earn stock awards as an Advanced Agent just for production. Additionally, just referring one or two agents to become an Advanced Agent has the ability to earn you even more stock and passive income. The possibilities are really in your hands. You can scale like a broker (except bypass the liability part) or continue your way to an icon top agent status in your sales business. Any of these can individually or collectively add to your potential net worth.

Ask yourself how much stock the company you currently produce for has given you each year. I'll bet the answer is zero. I know this because I've polled close to a thousand typical agents and they all say the same thing: "None – not even one stock award."

What if I told you every time you added an agent to grow your tribe, you could earn more public stock. This is a bonus on top of the game changer of mailbox money I mentioned in chapter 6. You see, every Advanced Agent has more than one way to earn income and create an exit strategy for retirement.

Would you start to imagine maybe there was a way to exit real estate in the future with a possible retirement and more money in hand? We all know there are no guarantees in life, as none of us are even promised tomorrow. But there is a heck of a lot better chance of gaining something while positioning yourself as an Advanced Agent.

Let us share with you the way you can keep more agents happy and have them be successful with equity ownership, including your own. Let's connect on a call and reserve a time that works for you by going to www.MeetupwithRick.com

CASE STUDY

Dr. Hank

Prior to seeing the vision as an Advanced Agent, Dr. Hank was both successful in the mortgage industry as well as becoming a partner in a brokerage paying 100% commissions to the agents, minus a moderate transaction fee. He was successful in helping grow the agency to several hundred agents, a task in itself that took several years. The biggest issue was they were simply restricted by the geographic barriers where the brokerage was located. This issue, coupled with very small profit margins of running a 100% agency, made it hard to support and have any value proposition beyond commissions splits. We have a saying in our business: "You can't cash a percentage." In other words, a 100% of nothing is still nothing.

As an owner or broker, you can only offer what you can afford. This can limit hiring, training, administrative support, insurance, and the entire value proposition. The flat fee model can be beneficial for a very experienced agent who can produce a source of leads. However, it is not as lucrative for owners due to the massive amount of overhead needed to keep operations running.

After a mutual friend arranged a discovery call, we formulated a plan to grow not just in his local market but nationwide and internationally. What we determined was that most agents really weren't at 100% due to the out-of-pocket expenses they needed to pay for the technology, tools, and marketing expenses out of their own pockets.

Dr. Hank, within a short 12-month period, has been able to offer a value proposition much more attractive for higher producers than even a 100% commission at his previously owned company. Currently, Dr. Hank has a business with over 40 agents (which he does not have to manage, train, or be liable for). This is only 10% compared to his previous brokerage but his net take-home is two times higher, far less work, and almost zero overhead. He's growing a net worth of stock awards by production at a steady pace and continues to offer greater value of two agents by referring them to become Advanced Agents with him.

Call to Action----> To learn more about how to offer an extreme amount of value to agents to both attract and retain them, let's hop on a discovery call. Visit www.MeetupwithRick.com

Conclusion: **The Future of Real Estate**

How many of you can remember back to when the MLS listings were delivered in the form of a big, thick, Yellow Pages type of book? Most of you probably can't or don't want to remember that far back or perhaps you weren't even an agent back then. The reality was that it took real work to find properties for clients or do the refined and filtered searches that we are all accustomed to now in this online world. We would most likely have to wait for the next publication cycle to place our seller listings in the book; none of this instant uploading via the internet. It goes without saying that has all changed. The future of many industries are changing and being disrupted right before our eyes. The question is if you are prepared for the shift in our industry.

The general public has had access to almost anything and everything at

their fingertips since the creation of the internet and the invention of smart devices (i.e. phones and tablets). They now have access to the same MLS information we have as professionals in the business. This sense of instant gratification has become the new norm for all of us and it seems like something we all take for granted in our daily lives. The way commerce is transacted has changed so fast over the last five years and it's only becoming more streamlined. There is no turning back. It's amazing how much technology has disrupted every sphere of business, most notably, brick and mortar business are being squeezed out by click and order and more efficient, online, cloud-based models. In case you haven't noticed it yet you soon will for sure.

How many of you remember Blockbuster movie rentals? We used to go down and try to be first in line rent a single copy of the latest releases. I remember several times going there on a Friday evening to rent the latest "blockbuster" release only to be beat out by someone who nabbed it before me. Bummer, right? Well, guess what? Now I just go on a cloud-based website and download it from the convenience from my own home, with no gas, no lines, no fuss, and bam – instant gratification!

I have to tell you, former Blockbuster workers all over the world must cringe every time they hear the words "online streaming" and "on-demand" or anything "cloud-based." That's because back in 2000, Reed Hastings approached former Blockbuster CEO John Antioco and asked him for $50 Million to give away the company he founded — Netflix. Reed actually got on a plane and flew to Dallas, Texas to court the Blockbuster CEO.

Blockbuster, thinking that it was a "very small niche business," ended the negotiations and didn't embrace the disruptive technology of Netflix, which at the time was just a DVD mailing service. Reed Hastings has been known to say, "Antioco – of Blockbuster nearly laughed him out of his offices."

Netflix rapidly scaled in market adoption and after just a few short years became worth the same as the television network CBS. The cloud-based model Netflix has now skyrocketed past the television network owner with a current market valuation of over $80 Billion. Netflix has also reached well over 50 million subscribers of its paid service and is available in 40 countries.

This isn't the first time that people and companies missed out on an opportunity that could have shifted their very own business world. There have been others, including Verizon shunning Apple for the first model of the iPhone, Comcast foregoing Disney, and AOL merging with Time Warner instead of AT&T. Perhaps the company that made the biggest blunder in on line history is Yahoo, which had chances to buy both Google and Facebook.

Conclusion:

Our industry will face a number of fundamental shifts that will shapes its future, just like the ridesharing giant Uber, e-commerce giant Amazon, and hospitality giant Airbnb. The real estate industry is being transformed by online cloud-based companies who are the innovators like Netflix.

We are already aware that home buyers research 90% of their buying decision online before they even contact an agent of choice. The days of agents needing a brick and mortar office to meet clients and conduct business is becoming extinct. Our industry will succumb to technology just as Blockbuster did. The cost savings model of online, cloud-based tools strips the physical model of far less cost and doing business with more efficiency. There is no need for multiple managing brokers in one organization or duplicating administrative staff, copiers, signage, or anything else for that matter. It is all done efficiently under one umbrella in the cloud, not to mention all of the online options for agents to nurture client relations via email, Docu-Sign, virtual conferencing, and paperless pipelines. A cloud-based or virtual office will become the new norm for many.

While many of the trends are already evident, there's a natural tenancy to underestimate how much and how fast our industry will change. Most people are too busy drinking their own Kool-Aid to even notice. Embracing the future now will set how the operating landscape of our industry takes shape. It will be the early adopter owners, brokers, and agents who prepare for these changes ahead of time who can turn them into fostering a competitive advantage.

I will say that "Managing your business and having vision within your business are two separate things." Collaborating with technology, innovation, and value will be the key for all of our sustainability.

Focusing this book on the practical implementation of the what and how is easy, but we only work with people who can see the changes happening and are on the same wavelength as us. We invest effort and resources in partnering with others and are therefore limited to who we can work with. we are looking for people that are looking for us.

If you're tired of living in the status quo, frustrated with doing things the way they've always been done, and not really gaining traction on where you want to go, then a strategy session makes sense for both of us to explore the opportunities available to change your business and life for the better.

Our mission is "To inspire and empower the real estate agent by propelling them to fulfil their maximum potential." If you're curious, intrigued and interested in exactly how to achieve the same results as the people you've just read about, you can also visit us online at www.theadvancedagent.com

My Network was created to support the Advanced to inspire and empower the real estate professional who essentially systematize all of the successes we've shared with you, making it easier to adopt many of our strategies.

Alternatively, you can reach me to schedule a call at www.MeetupwithRick.com and explore the possibilities for you to become an Advanced Agent. We look forward to meeting you.

Before you close this chapter, take a moment to imagine what more time and money would mean in your life and those your care about. If you have made it this far congratulations! You are far beyond the status quo. What it takes from here is for you to become a leader and to break the cycle of mediocrity.

As always, To Positive Success

Made in the USA
Las Vegas, NV
10 November 2026

57845502R00050